Kennedy's BIG Visit

Daphne Brooks

Copyright © 2015 Daphne Brooks.

All rights reserved. No part of this book may be used or reproduced by any means, graphic, electronic, or mechanical, including photocopying, recording, taping or by any information storage retrieval system without the written permission of the publisher except in the case of brief quotations embodied in critical articles and reviews.

Archway Publishing books may be ordered through booksellers or by contacting:

Archway Publishing
1663 Liberty Drive
Bloomington, IN 47403
www.archwaypublishing.com
1 (888) 242-5904

Because of the dynamic nature of the Internet, any web addresses or links contained in this book may have changed since publication and may no longer be valid. The views expressed in this work are solely those of the author and do not necessarily reflect the views of the publisher, and the publisher hereby disclaims any responsibility for them.

Any people depicted in stock imagery provided by Thinkstock are models, and such images are being used for illustrative purposes only.
Certain stock imagery © Thinkstock.

ISBN: 978-1-4808-1783-8 (sc)
ISBN: 978-1-4808-1784-5 (hc)
ISBN: 978-1-4808-1785-2 (e)

Print information available on the last page.

Archway Publishing rev. date: 04/28/2015

This book is dedicated to all the children with incarcerated fathers and their guardians that make their relationship possible.

It's Saturday morning and Kennedy is so anxious to visit her dad. She never wakes up early but today is different. She wakes up at 6:00 am. She runs to her mother's room to wake her. "Mommy wake up, we are going to be late" says Kennedy.

"Kennedy, you are so loud and up so early" Daphne says with a smile. "Did you wash your face and brush your teeth, you might make daddy pass out with that stinky breath" her mother said as she tickled her on the bed.

Kennedy and Daphne go into the bathroom to brush their teeth and wash their face. "Kennedy, make sure you use mouthwash for the extra freshness" says her mother. Once Kennedy finishes in the bathroom, she goes to her room to get dressed. "I want to look pretty for Daddy" Kennedy says. She put on a princess dress with play shoes, her mother tells her to change.

Then she puts on the biggest tutu she can find with the shirt to match, her mother shakes her head no. "Mommy, my dad said I am a princess. Princesses wear poufy dresses and heels" Kennedy says. "You are our princess but you know there are dress rules where daddy is" her mother said "OK" Kennedy said with a sad face. "I will let you pick out your own clothes, if you put something on that is not appropriate, mommy will have to choose OK" her mother said "Ok mommy, and I will put on something nice" Kennedy said

"Kennedy, are you hungry?" her mother asks. "No" Kennedy responds. Daphne knows that Kennedy is indeed hungry but is too anxious to eat. If she doesn't eat, she is going to want everything in the vending machine.

"Kennedy, come eat a little bowl of oatmeal, you are going to get sick if you don't eat and then we won't be able to see Daddy" her mother says. Kennedy comes downstairs dressed and ready to eat a small bowl of oatmeal. Daphne joins her at the table. Kennedy is trying to eat extra fast so they can leave. "Slow down Kennedy before you choke." Her mother said with a smile.

"You know you are the smartest most beautiful daughter in the whole wide world Kennedy" Daphne says "Yes Mom and you are the best Mommy in the whole wide world" Kennedy says. They hug and give each other a kiss. "Kennedy, don't let mommy forget to mail daddy's letters on our way there. I sent him your last progress report." says her mother "OK mommy" says Kennedy

"Are we there yet?" Kennedy asks. "No Kennedy, if you keep asking, it makes the ride longer Remember, Daddy is not going anywhere, he will be there when we get there, OK" her mother says Kennedy continues to play with her tablet.

"Inmate number" says the correctional officer "EXY417" Daphne says. Daphne gives the correctional officer her photo Id and Kennedy's birth certificate. "Mommy let's get the locker" Kennedy says "Slow down Kennedy, we have to sign in first.

Daphne pays the clerk to get a key to the locker. Daphne puts their jackets and her handbag in the locker.
"Scott" yells the correctional officer "Mom, come on, they called Daddy" Kennedy says.

"I'm hungry, Princess, you ready to eat" Kenta says "No daddy, I just want like some popcorn and a soda" Kennedy says "No soda, just a juice" Daphne says.

"Daddy can I play outside on the sliding board"? "Come on, it's nice outside, me and mommy can sit on the bench" Daphne says

"Daphne, thank you for coming up and bringing our daughter to see me. The hardest part about being in here is being away from you and our princess." Kenta says

"I just hope you learned your lesson. All that expensive stuff you put your freedom on the line for is not worth you being away from us. I know you grew up poor and you want to provide a better life for Kennedy but that's why I went to college. I am trying to graduate and be in a career by the time you come home. I don't want to put that added pressure on you. I appreciate everything that you do but you have to start from the bottom. Kennedy is more concerned with your presence than the presents you bring home. You can take her to the dollar store and get her a bunch of junk for $5.00. She is going to be happy. I grew up with a mom and step-dad that spoiled me but I still remained close to my drug addicted father. He never had any money to give me but he always came around. A parent's presence is very important in a child's life. I bring her up here to see you because I know how important that is to her." Daphne says. "It's a lot of guys in here who have not seen their kids in years" Kenta says. "Some parents don't want to subject their children to this which is understandable but that presence piece is very important" Daphne says." You know Daph, that's why I chose you. You showed me a different life. I didn't really follow everything but, you are really something special, you know that" Kenta says. Daphne smiles.

The visit is coming to an end. This is usually the saddest part of the visit. Everybody in the visiting room began to hug and kiss their loved ones goodbye "OK, princess, Daddy will see you next week, be good in school, say no to drugs, listen to mommy, stay away from boys and strangers. Daddy love you, give Daddy kiss" says Kenta. Kennedy kisses her Daddy. Kennedy is teary eyed but she doesn't cry because she knows Daddy will be home soon.

Days past and Kennedy is anticipating her next visit to see Daddy. It's a hot day and all of Kennedy's friends are outside playing. "Hey Kennedy." Kennedy and her friends began to play hide and go seek immediately. Kennedy always seem to think that she can hide behind the same tree every time they play. Her friend Kendall always seems to find her. While they are playing hopscotch, Kennedy's mother gives everybody some homemade lemonade freeze pops. Kennedy's friends thought it was the best lemonade in the whole world. They always tried to get seconds. The lemonade pops was a sign that Kennedy would be going in to eat dinner soon.

Daphne calls Kennedy in to eat "Kennedy, it's time to eat" "Bye guys, I will see yall tomorrow" Kennedy says to her friends. Kennedy washed her hands and sits at the table. 'Say the grace Kennedy" Daphne says "God is great, God is good, thank you for this food we about to receive and God please bring my Daddy home, Amen. Mommy, do you think God will bring Daddy home soon?" Kennedy asks. "Of course God will bring Daddy home. Remember when Mommy and Daddy talked to you about being punished for doing bad things and making bad choices?" Daphne says. "Yes" Kennedy says. "Well, daddy is being punished for making bad choices. Daddy said he learned his lesson and he will not go away from us ever again OK" Daphne said "Ok mommy" Kennedy said.

THE DAY BEFORE THE NEXT VISIT

Kennedy is in her room trying to decide what she wants to wear tomorrow. Her dad told her they are having family day at the prison. Last year, he won the potato sack race. Kennedy hopes he wins again so she can get another gift. Tomorrow, she is going to tell her dad that she wants another Ballerina painting delivered by Kennedy's Treasures. Kennedy gets a little exhausted and decided to go downstairs on the couch with her mother. Just as she began to nod off, the doorbell rang. Her mother got up and answered the door. When her mother opened the door, she heard her say "OMG, I can't believe this." Very excitedly. When Kennedy turned around, she jumped up and ran to the door

"Daddy I always ask God to bring you home, did you hear me? Kennedy asks "No princess but I promise to never go away from you ever again" Kenta said.

CPSIA information can be obtained
at www.ICGtesting.com
Printed in the USA
LVHW071052200321
681766LV00014BA/437